W9-BXD-452

APPS

FROM CONCEPT TO CONSUMER

BY JOSH GREGORY

CHILDREN'S PRESS®

An Imprint of Scholastic Inc.
New York   Toronto   London   Auckland   Sydney
Mexico City   New Delhi   Hong Kong
Danbury, Connecticut

CONTENT CONSULTANT: Nick Leonard, User Experience Designer, Fuzzy Math

PHOTOGRAPHS ©: Alamy Images: 19 (Anatolii Babii), 31 bottom (AugustSnow), 12 (Blend Images), 24 bottom (Ian Dagnall), 51 top (Jake Charles), 3, 58 (Jeffrey Blackler), 24 top, 25 top (Kumar Sriskandan), 39 top (PhotoAlto), 10 (Pictorial Press Ltd), 53 (Radius Images), 52 (suedhang/Cultura Creative), 17 (Zuma Press, Inc.); AP Images: 11 top (Eric Risberg), 14 (John Everett/Houston Chronicle), 18 (Meigneux/SIPA), 4 left, 13 (TGPRN Bass Hotels & Resorts/ PRNewsFoto); Corbis Images/Piero Cruciatti/Demotix: 41; Dreamstime: 6; Getty Images: 54 bottom (Dieter Spannknebel), 25 bottom (Park Ji-Hwan/AFP), 50 bottom, 51 bottom (Romeo Gacad/AFP), 38 top (small_frog), 20 (Stephen Simpson); Media Bakery: 45 (Andersen Ross), 11 bottom (B2M Productions), 44 (Bernhard Classen), 30 (Leren Lu), 56 (MF), 29 (Nicole Hill), 28 (Roberto Westbrook), 32 (Sam Edwards), 38 bottom, 39 bottom (Steve Prezant); Nick Leonard: 42, 43; Shutterstock, Inc.: 15 (bokan), 27 (djile), 46 (dolphfyn), 40 (Edw), 55 (Evgeny Vasenev), 31 top (Johanna Goodyear), 23, 54 top (LDprod), 5 right, 48 (Monkey Business Images), cover (Nata-Lia), 37, 59 (Oleksiy Mark), 33 (Panom Pensawang), 4 right, 22, 50 top (Twin Design), 5 left, 36 (wavebreakmedia); The Image Works: 57 (Chris Fitzgerald), 9 (D. & P. Valenti/Classicstock), 16 (David Frazier), 34, 49 (Melanie Stetson Freeman/Christian Science Monitor), 26 (Richard B. Levine), 8 (SZ Photo).

LIBRARY OF CONGRESS CATALOGING-IN-PUBLICATION DATA
Gregory, Josh, author.
  Apps : from concept to consumer / by Josh Gregory.
    pages cm. — (Calling all innovators: a career for you)
  Summary: "Learn about the history of mobile apps and find out what it takes to make it in this exciting career field" — Provided by publisher.
  Audience: Age 9–12.
  Audience: Grades 4–6.
  Includes bibliographical references and index.
  ISBN 978-0-531-20539-6 (library binding : alk. paper) — ISBN 978-0-531-21236-3 (pbk. : alk. paper)
  1. Mobile computing — Juvenile literature. 2. Application software — Juvenile literature.
  3. Application software — Development — Vocational guidance — Juvenile literature. I. Title.
  QA76.59.G74 2015
  005.35023 — dc23   2014030460

All rights reserved. Published in 2015 by Children's Press, an imprint of Scholastic Inc.
Printed in the United States of America 113

3 4 5 6 7 8 9 10 R 24 23 22 21 20 19 18 17 16 15

Science, technology, engineering, arts, and math are the fields that drive innovation. Whether they are finding ways to make our lives easier or developing the latest entertainment, the people who work in these fields are changing the world for the better. Do you have what it takes to join the ranks of today's greatest innovators? Read on to discover if a career in the exciting world of app development is for you.

TABLE *of* CONTENTS

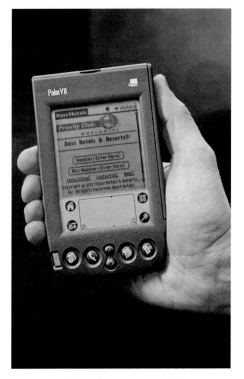

Personal digital assistants used apps similar to those on today's smartphones.

Today, there is an incredible variety of apps to choose from.

Designers discuss plans for a new app.

It is easy to get started in the world of app building.

People can accomplish all kinds of tasks by using a single pocket-sized device.

1

IN THE PALM OF YOUR HAND

I magine you're on vacation in a city you've never visited before. You might need a map to find your way around. You might also want to look up information about interesting places to visit. Where are the best restaurants? Where can you find interesting stores to buy souvenirs for your friends back home? Maybe you'd like to buy tickets to a play or take a photo of a famous landmark. Today, you can do all of these things by simply pulling out your smartphone and opening the right app. This wasn't always the case, though. Originally, mobile devices could do little more than make telephone calls. Modern smartphones are powerful handheld computers. They can do almost anything an app **developer** can dream up!

EARLY DEVICES

1984	1994	2002	2007
Motorola's DynaTAC 8000X is released, becoming the first commercially available cell phone.	The IBM Simon becomes the first smartphone to hit stores.	The BlackBerry 5810 changes the way people use apps on handheld devices.	Apple's iPhone helps turn smartphones into common household items.

PUTTING COMPUTERS TO WORK

The word *app* is short for "application." An application is a computer program that enables users to complete any number of tasks. There are applications for browsing the Internet, checking e-mail, and typing documents. Video games are applications. So are the programs people use to watch videos or listen to music on a computer.

Unlike today's mobile apps, the earliest computer programs were far from portable. They were designed for large computer systems in places such as businesses and schools. The first computers, developed in the mid-20th century, were so large that they filled entire rooms. In those days, the idea of a computer that could fit in your pocket probably seemed like something from a science-fiction movie.

A worker sits at the center of operations of a computer called UNIVAC in Frankfurt, Germany, in 1956.

WHITE-ON-BLACK
SCREEN DISPLAY

Early home computers often had simple games to play.

APPS AT HOME

Computer technology quickly became smaller and more powerful. By the late 1970s, personal computers such as the Apple II had become popular for home use. With more and more people learning how to use computers, the demand for applications began to grow. At first, users had to use **programming languages** to create their own **software**. Before long, however, there were a variety of programs available for people to purchase. Inexperienced users with no programming knowledge could buy these applications and install them on their personal computers. In addition, popular **operating systems** such as Microsoft Windows and Apple's Mac OS came with a number of useful built-in apps, such as calculators, address books, and simple art programs. By the mid-1990s, computer applications had become a part of daily life for millions of people around the world.

FIRST THINGS FIRST

Inventor Alexander Graham Bell made the world's first telephone call in 1876.

MAKING CALLS

Today, a mobile phone can instantly connect you with someone halfway around the world at the touch of a button, no matter where you are. You can text, send an e-mail, video chat, or use a number of other options. But communication possibilities have not always been so numerous. The first telephone was invented in 1876. For almost 100 years afterward, telephones could only connect to communications **networks** through wires.

OVER THE AIR

In 1973, Motorola **engineer** Martin Cooper made the first mobile phone call. Cooper and his fellow researchers had discovered a way to send telephone signals using radio waves. With a phone that weighed roughly 2 pounds (0.9 kilogram), Cooper demonstrated the new wireless technology to a group of reporters. He did so by making a call to a rival inventor at Bell Labs to announce Motorola's victory in the race to build the first mobile phone. The press was amazed by the new technology, but it was not until the 1980s that portable wireless phones were introduced to the public.

Martin Cooper holds up a DynaTAC cellular phone.

PHONES ON THE GO

The first commercially available portable **cellular** phone, Motorola's DynaTAC 8000X, went on sale in 1984. It was extremely large and heavy compared to modern cell phones. It was also very expensive, with a price tag of almost $4,000. Users could do little more than make basic telephone calls with the device. Because of their size and expense, the DynaTACs and other early cell phones were mainly used by traveling businesspeople, who carried them in their briefcases.

POCKET SIZE

Over time, mobile phones became smaller and more affordable, making them more appealing for everyday use. In 1996, Motorola introduced the first "flip phone." This design allowed the phone to fold in half, making it easy to fit into a pocket or purse. Two years later, Nokia released the first mobile phone without an antenna sticking out of the top. This meant cell phones took up even less space, making them more portable. ✹

The ability to fold a phone in half made cell phones more mobile than ever.

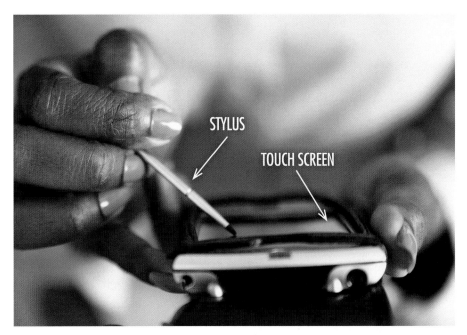
STYLUS

TOUCH SCREEN

Touch-screen PDAs helped pave the way for smartphones.

GETTING SMARTER

In the 1990s, computer companies began selling handheld devices called personal digital assistants, or PDAs. Early PDAs were equipped with simple, one-color touch screens and apps such as an address book, a calendar, and a notepad. Most people who used them were businesspeople who needed to access scheduling and contact information on the go.

Over time, PDAs became more powerful, adding features such as full-color graphics and more sensitive touch screens. Software developers took advantage of these features to create more apps using mobile operating systems such as Palm OS and Microsoft Windows CE. By the late 1990s, PDA owners could use their devices to play music and video files, browse and edit documents, and even take digital photos using built-in cameras. More and more people were starting to see the appeal of handheld computers.

CUTTING THE CORD

Connecting to the Internet is an important part of the majority of today's most popular mobile apps. Like making a telephone call, getting online once required access to a wired network. But in the 1990s, mobile phones and PDAs began using cellular networks to provide limited Internet access on the go.

One of the first successful handheld devices to offer wireless Internet service was the Palm VII. For a monthly fee, users could send and receive e-mail and access simplified versions of several popular Web sites through built-in apps. While users could not access full Web pages or download files, they could look up information such as sports scores, weather forecasts, or stock prices even when they were away from their desks. This was still a far cry from the powerful e-mail and Web browser apps of modern devices, but it was a major step forward.

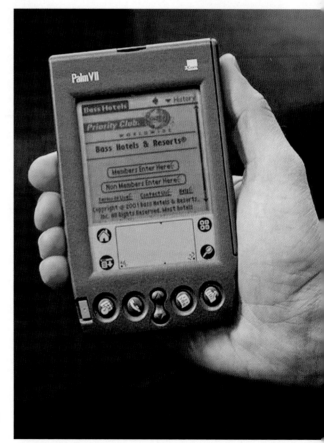

The Palm VII showed how useful it could be to have Internet access on the go.

The Simon was designed as a kind of portable office computer.

SIMPLE SIMON

In 1992, engineers from the computer manufacturer IBM unveiled a new mobile device at a computer show in Las Vegas, Nevada. Like a PDA, it featured a touch screen and a number of simple, built-in apps. However, unlike a PDA, this unique device was also a cellular phone. Called Simon, it was the world's first smartphone.

THE FIRST PHONE APPS

Much like a modern smartphone, the Simon had a home screen with a number of icons to represent different apps. Touching an icon would open the app. The device's built-in programs included a calendar, a to-do list, and even a simple game called Scramble.

EXPANDED OPTIONS

The Simon could not simply connect to the Internet and download new apps the way a modern smartphone can. Instead, it was equipped with an expansion slot. Users could plug in cards containing new apps, such as a music player or basic accounting software. The expansion slot could also be used to connect additional **hardware**, such as a digital camera.

Today's smartphones have many of the same capabilities found on the Simon.

AHEAD OF ITS TIME

With a battery life of less than an hour and a price of around $900, the Simon was not a practical device for most users. As a result, it didn't quite take off as the next big thing. It was only available for around six months. Roughly 50,000 Simons were sold during this time, which is insignificant compared to the millions of smartphones sold in the same amount of time today. However, many of this remarkably forward-thinking device's features and apps would come to be a standard part of mobile phones years later. ✹

THE BLACKBERRY BOOM

In 2002, the Canadian company Research in Motion released the BlackBerry 5810, the latest in its BlackBerry line of PDAs. Like previous BlackBerry devices, it featured a small keyboard for typing messages, a number of built-in apps, and wireless Internet access. However, unlike other PDAs, it also allowed users to make telephone calls. The combination of these features made it one of the first modern smartphones. The BlackBerry 5810 was an immediate success. Like similar devices, it was aimed mainly at businesspeople at first. However, it soon began to catch on among the general public, who enjoyed being able to stay connected to the Internet wherever they went.

BlackBerry devices were popular business tools for many years.

THE BIRTH OF THE IPHONE

Smartphones became fairly popular in the years following the BlackBerry's debut. However, most available smartphone apps were still focused on business-related tasks, such as accounting and scheduling. In addition, the apps often relied on complicated **interfaces** that were difficult for beginners to get used to.

That all changed in 2007, when Apple Inc. unveiled the iPhone. The iPhone combined the useful features of earlier smartphones with the music, video, and other entertainment options of Apple's hugely popular iPod. It also offered a large, extremely responsive touch screen to control almost all of the phone's features. This helped create a much more user-friendly interface, compared to the complex combination of keyboards and small touch-responsive areas that other smartphones used.

Steve Jobs explains the capabilities of the iPhone at its unveiling in 2007.

STEVE JOBS

Steve Jobs founded Apple Inc. in the 1970s alongside engineer Steve Wozniak. Under Jobs's guidance, Apple introduced some of the first successful personal computers and grew to become one of the largest computer companies in the world. Jobs believed that tech devices should be visually appealing and easy to use, even for beginners. This philosophy helped lead Apple to enormous success in the 2000s with devices such as the iPod, iPhone, and iPad.

People line up to purchase iPhones outside a shop in Paris in 2007.

SMARTPHONE MANIA

The iPhone was a huge success. Its iOS operating system came with built-in apps for watching movies, listening to music, browsing the Internet, and much more. It wasn't just a phone or a practical business tool. It was also an entertaining toy and a great way to access the nearly limitless information of the Internet.

Apple's slick new device introduced millions of people to the usefulness of smartphones. Within months, other phone manufacturers began following the iPhone's lead with colorful, touch-driven interfaces and a focus on fun, creativity, and entertainment. Phones using Google's Android operating system debuted in 2008, helping spread the smartphone revolution even further.

SHOPPING SPREE

The potential for mobile apps reached a new level in 2008, when Apple's iOS App Store and Google's Android Market made their debuts. These services allowed users to purchase and download new apps over the Internet with a few simple touches.

Smartphone users were no longer limited to using the apps that came preinstalled on their phones. Anyone who had the necessary skills was free to create a new app and submit it to be posted on these online stores. This meant that any programmer with a unique idea could easily distribute his or her app to an audience of millions, so long as it met Apple's basic guidelines. With so many people looking for new ways to use their devices and so many creative minds hard at work on new projects, the number of available apps exploded. Within a year of its debut, the number of available apps on the App Store grew from about 500 to more than 50,000.

Services such as the iOS App Store have made it easy to find and download new apps for mobile devices such as the iPad.

Today, mobile apps are used by kids and adults alike.

2

AN AVALANCHE OF APPS

Picture your family sitting in the living room after dinner one evening. Each person is busy tapping and swiping on his or her mobile device. Your mom is following along with play-by-play reports of her favorite basketball team as she types an e-mail to your grandparents. Your older sister is reading movie reviews, checking showtimes, and texting with her friends to make plans for the night. Your baby brother is playing a game that helps him learn to read. Your dad has just finished booking flights for the upcoming family vacation, and now he is swiping through recipes in the latest issue of his favorite cooking magazine. Meanwhile, the whole family chats about their day. This sort of **multitasking** is just one of the many advantages provided by today's enormous variety of mobile apps.

TABLETS TAKE OFF

1987	2010	2011	2012
The first tablet computers go on sale.	Apple releases the iPad, helping popularize tablet computers.	Amazon debuts the Kindle Fire, which quickly becomes one of the most popular tablet computers.	Google releases its first Android-powered tablet, the Nexus 7.

UNLIMITED OPTIONS

Today, more than a billion people around the world use smartphones and other mobile devices. There are more than a million different apps available to download on dozens of different devices, with more apps being created every day. By 2014, more than 60 billion app downloads had been made through the iOS App Store. The Google Play store (formerly known as the Android Market) had also racked up more than 50 billion downloads in its app section.

Many of these apps are basic programs such as novelty sound effect generators or "flashlights" that cause a device's screen to display bright-white light. Others are more complex pieces of software that offer many of the same features as "full-sized" personal computer programs. Most mobile apps are inexpensive, costing only a few dollars. Many are even free. This encourages users to try out lots of different apps to see which ones they like best.

Apps serve countless purposes, from helping people keep in touch to predicting the weather.

TAP ICONS ON A SMARTPHONE TO OPEN APPS

Video-chatting apps can be used on most of today's phones and tablets.

STAYING IN TOUCH

Even as apps have made mobile devices capable of almost anything, many of the most popular apps are still focused on the same purpose for which the telephone was first invented: communication. Almost all mobile devices come with built-in apps for text messaging and e-mail. For those who want a more personal touch, video chatting has become a popular method of communicating with distant friends. Apps such as Skype and Apple's FaceTime provide a simple way for users to talk face-to-face with people all over the world.

Social media apps have long been some of the most popular downloads at online app stores. Long-running social networks such as Twitter and Facebook have become even more popular as the use of mobile devices has spread. Social media apps such as Instagram and Vine give users an easy way to take photos or videos with their devices and post them online immediately.

MODERN MARVEL

TRIUMPH OF TABLETS

Smartphones aren't the only devices people can use to run their favorite apps. Tablet computers have become an extremely popular alternative for app users. Larger screens make it easier to read magazines and newspapers or to watch videos, and more powerful computer hardware makes tablets capable of displaying the latest 3D graphics. These features also give app developers the freedom to create programs that might not work on a smartphone.

FIRST STEPS

The year 1987 saw the release of the first portable tablet computers. The Z88 tablet, by Cambridge Research, had a very small, single-color screen and was controlled entirely through a keyboard. The Write-Top, by Linus Technologies, relied on a **stylus**-based touch screen instead of a keyboard. These devices did not offer nearly as many features as we have come to expect from modern tablet computers. Instead, they were used mainly for typing or writing documents.

The Z88 had a much smaller screen than today's tablets.

Customers try out iPads at an Apple Store.

TABLETS TAKE OFF

Though tablet computers have been around for a long time, they have only become popular in recent years. It was not until Apple introduced the iPad in 2010 that tablet sales took off among the general public. Because the new device used the same iOS operating system as the iPhone, it was instantly familiar to millions of users. In addition, it could run all of the same apps iPhone owners already used on their phones. In 2009, the year before the iPad was released, around 2 million tablet computers were sold. By 2013,

annual sales had increased to almost 200 million. The iPad's popularity led to a wide variety of other tablets hitting the market. Many of the most popular tablets, including Amazon's Kindle Fire and Samsung's Galaxy Tab, use the Android operating system, making them compatible with the huge range of apps designed for Android smartphones.

BLURRED LINES

Mobile device manufacturers have begun to introduce slightly smaller tablets, such as the iPad Mini and Google's Nexus 7. These devices have gained popularity for their balance between the large screen of a tablet and the portability of a phone. At the same time, phones with larger screens are also becoming popular. Many experts predict that these larger phones will soon take the place of tablets for many users. ☀

Many companies produce small and large versions of their tablets.

DETACHABLE
KEYBOARD →

Some users prefer using a keyboard to typing on a touch screen.

A PORTABLE OFFICE

Today, there is an incredible range of productivity apps available for download, and many people no longer need to be at a desk to get work done. Microsoft Office and Apple's iWork both offer mobile versions of their software. These apps offer many of the same options as the traditional PC and Macintosh programs they are based on. Users can create and edit text documents, spreadsheets, slide shows, and more. People can even connect keyboards to their devices for easier typing.

Apps such as Dropbox and Google Drive enable workers to share files with coworkers. That way they can collaborate to create documents. If they need to discuss something, they might hold an online video meeting with an app like Cisco WebEx Meetings. Workers can even access a desktop computer from afar by logging into an app such as Microsoft Remote Desktop. Using such apps in combination with each other can be almost the same as being in a real office.

MAKING SOME NOISE

If you're interested in making music on a mobile device, there are plenty of apps that can do the job. Apple's GarageBand gives users access to virtual drums, keyboards, and guitars that can be used to build songs. Native Instruments' iMaschine is a portable version of the popular Maschine audio software. It allows users to create beats using a variety of built-in drum machines and synthesizers. Traktor DJ provides portable tools for mixing and remixing tracks to create the perfect groove. If you would rather write music to play on live instruments, you might check out Notion, a popular app for composing sheet music. Once you've created the perfect song, try uploading it with an app like SoundCloud so others can listen.

If you'd rather just listen to your favorite songs, there are plenty of options to choose from. Spotify and Beats Music are services that allow users to browse and stream from a library containing millions of songs. For people who don't know exactly what songs they want to listen to, apps such as Pandora Radio and iHeartRadio offer customized streaming radio services. And if you ever hear a great new song on the radio, at a party, or on your favorite TV show, you might use an app called Shazam to find out what it's called.

A range of music apps allow you to create, listen to, and share your own music.

A LIBRARY ON THE GO

With the help of an e-reader app, it's easy to carry thousands of books with you wherever you go. Some e-reader apps, such as Apple's iBooks, Amazon's Kindle, or Google Play Books, are connected to online bookstores where you can purchase something to read and link it to an account. Then you can access the books from any of your devices. Other e-readers connect to public libraries and allow users to "check out" e-books using their library cards. If you don't have time to read, you might be interested in an app such as Audible, which allows you to download and listen to audiobooks. Once you've read a few books, you might want to share your thoughts and get ideas for new things to read by using Goodreads, a popular social app for book fans.

Books aren't the only things to read on your mobile device. Almost all major magazines and newspapers offer mobile versions. Many times, these apps have features that wouldn't be possible in a paper version, such as built-in audio and video, Web links, and other interactive content.

An e-reader app makes it easy to find, buy, borrow, and read books without ever leaving home.

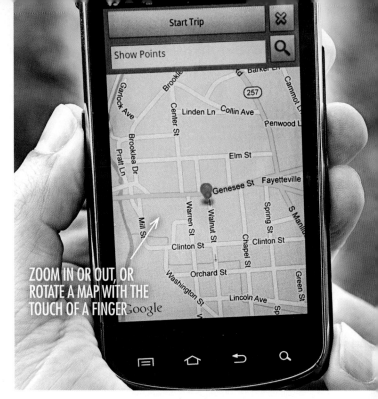

Map apps can provide different directions depending on whether you are driving, walking, or using public transportation.

NEVER GET LOST AGAIN

Most modern mobile devices have built-in **GPS** service. Many apps take advantage of this feature to help users find their way around, no matter where they are. For example, Google and Apple both offer powerful map apps. With a single touch, you can instantly see a map of the area you are in. As you move around, the map tracks your location. If you want to get somewhere in particular, simply type in the address and ask for directions. Your device will tell you how to reach your destination, step by step.

If you aren't quite sure where you want to go, you might use an app like Urbanspoon or Yelp. These apps use GPS to find out where you are, then search for nearby restaurants and other businesses. For example, you might want to look for a nearby Chinese restaurant. You can search to see what your options are. Once you've decided on a destination, simply tap on the name or address to get directions from your map app.

FROM THIS TO THAT

TAPPING AND SWIPING

Most smartphones and tablets have very few buttons built into them. Today's mobile devices are controlled almost exclusively with touch screens. Users control apps by tapping, swiping, and using a variety of other finger movements directly on the screen. This might seem like a very modern way of operating an electronic device. However, the earliest touch screens were actually invented decades ago.

ONE TOUCH AT A TIME

In 1965, a British engineer named E. A. Johnson developed the first capacitive touch screen. When a finger touches this type of screen, it **conducts** an electrical signal.

This tells the screen where it was touched. Unlike the touch screens used in most modern devices, Johnson's screen could only register a single touch at a time. This means that movements such as pinching or swiping the screen did not do anything. Despite these limitations, Johnson's invention was used for devices that track the flight paths of airplanes until the late 1990s.

THE RESISTANCE

In the early 1970s, a team led by Dr. G. Samuel Hurst invented the resistive touch screen. Instead of registering electrical signals from the touch of skin, this new

Devices are controlled through swipes, pinches, or a simple tap.

The small tip of a stylus can be used for more precise control.

type of screen responded to pressure. This meant that either a finger or a stylus could be used to register touches. Less expensive to produce than capacitive screens, resistive touch screens were used in a variety of devices throughout the following decades.

MULTITOUCH MAGIC

Multitouch technology got its start in 1982. That year, University of Toronto researcher Nimish Mehta constructed a glass surface that could register more than one touch at a time. By 1984, researchers at Bell Labs had applied similar concepts to a computer screen. Users could perform different movements with their fingers to change graphics on the screen.

TOUCH TAKES OFF

Simple, resistive touch screens first became a part of mobile phones with IBM's Simon phone in 1992. From then on, touch screens slowly became a bigger and bigger part of phone and PDA technology. Finally, the 2007 release of Apple's iPhone showed that touch screens were here to stay. The device's capacitive, multitouch screen was a big part of its success, and it forever changed the way people interacted with apps. ✳

Modern devices incorporate many different types of touch commands.

Video-streaming apps offer movies and TV shows for people of all ages.

ENDLESS ENTERTAINMENT

Thanks to the huge variety of video streaming options available today, app users will never run out of new things to watch on their devices. Whether you want to watch your favorite band's newest music video, a live sporting event, or the year's biggest Hollywood blockbuster, there are services that provide what you're looking for. Some streaming apps, such as YouTube, offer content uploaded by users. They are free for anyone to access. Services such as Netflix and Hulu Plus offer a wide variety of television shows and movies. They usually require a monthly fee to use. Other streaming services focus on specialized types of content. For example, Twitch is a popular app for streaming footage of video games, while Crunchyroll focuses on anime. Most TV channels, including HBO, NBC, and Cartoon Network, also offer apps that can be used to stream their shows. Most professional sports leagues also offer subscription-based video streaming apps.

GAME ON!

From the very beginning, video games have ranked among the most successful apps available. Many game apps are designed especially with smartphones and tablets in mind. They offer simple, touch-based controls and the type of gameplay that is best suited to short bursts of fun. This makes mobile games perfect for times when users need to kill a few minutes while standing in line or waiting to meet a friend. Some of the most popular examples include the *Angry Birds* and *Temple Run* series, which have each racked up more than a billion downloads.

Some mobile games are even more ambitious. *Minecraft: Pocket Edition*, which is based on a complex game originally developed for PCs and home game consoles, was the most successful mobile app of 2013. And the *Infinity Blade* series has pushed the visuals of mobile games to a whole new level with its incredible 3D graphics.

DONG NGUYEN

In April 2013, app developer Dong Nguyen uploaded a simple game called *Flappy Bird* to app stores. Nguyen planned his game to be extremely simple, yet hard to put down. Players would just tap on their phone screens to control the flight of a cartoon bird and avoid obstacles. At first, few people downloaded it. But in early 2014, the game became a **viral** sensation. As tens of millions of people downloaded the addictive game, Nguyen was earning as much as $50,000 a day. He was surprised by his sudden fame. Unhappy with how much attention he was getting, he decided to remove the game from app stores. However, he is hard at work on several new mobile games.

Some game apps encourage users to create digital art.

33

A team of designers takes a look at how an app is working on a smartphone.

CHAPTER THREE

CRAFTING A CAREER

Mobile app development is a rapidly growing field. Every day, more people are replacing their laptop and desktop PCs with smartphones, tablets, and other mobile devices, and the next big app success is only an idea away. Many of the apps released by big companies such as Google, Apple, or Facebook are developed and maintained by large teams of experts, each with his or her own expertise in a specific aspect of app development. However, these aren't the only apps out there. Small teams or even individual developers working in their spare time have created many successful apps. Anyone with creativity, skill, and motivation can make the next big thing in the app world.

OPEN FOR BUSINESS

July 2008	Oct. 2008	Oct. 2010	March 2011
Apple launches the iOS App Store.	Google launches the Android Market, which is renamed Google Play in 2012.	Microsoft launches the Windows Phone Store.	Amazon.com begins selling Android apps for use on its own devices.

DARING DEVELOPERS

People who think up ideas and plan out new apps are called developers. Every new app has at least one developer behind it, and many apps are created by groups of developers working together. A developer's job begins with a basic idea for a new type of app. From there, he or she thinks of different features that the app will have and decides how these features will fit together.

When developers are working as part of a larger team, they might provide instructions to other team members, such as artists or designers. As the project moves forward, they make sure their initial ideas are working the way they'd planned and make any necessary changes to the app. Some teams have a specific project manager or leader who is placed in charge of organizing and making sure tasks are completed.

Developers work to come up with ideas no one else has thought of yet.

Designers try to make sure an app works well and looks nice on a variety of devices.

CREATING AN EXPERIENCE

Some development teams employ specialized workers to design an app's user interface (UI) or user experience (UX). The UI is the way a user interacts with an app. It includes the types of touch commands used to control an app, the arrangement of elements on a screen, and the way different screens in an app are linked together. UI designers help make apps easy to use. They try to fit all of the necessary features together in a way that is not too complicated for a user to understand.

UX designers fine-tune the overall experience a user has with an app. They make sure an app's visuals, sounds, UI, and features work together to give users a satisfying feeling. For example, a UI designer might arrange the buttons in an app, while a UX designer might decide the color and shape of the buttons and the sound effect they produce when tapped. UX designers often conduct research, asking people to test an app to find out how they feel about it and whether they have a difficult time learning to operate it. Some designers might work on both UI and UX, while larger teams might have separate workers for each.

THE ARTISTIC SIDE

THE COLOR AND THE SHAPE

A great app is more than just features and content. Today's mobile devices come equipped with full-color, high-definition screens. Colorful, creative graphics can help an app stand out from the competition. Many app development teams employ graphic designers to create everything from logos, buttons, and icons to eye-catching background screens and other images. Graphic designers have a strong understanding of the way different colors, shapes, and fonts work together to appeal to the app's intended audience. They use a variety of software to help them design an app's graphics and text. Some also create drawings and illustrations by hand.

A graphic designer chooses just the right colors for a project.

MUSIC MAKERS

Many apps feature a variety of music and sound effects to enhance the user's experience. Development teams might enlist the services of a professional composer to help them create the right music for their project. Music and sound effects for apps are usually created using computer software rather than live instruments. Music software allows composers to write, edit, and record their work using synthetic, or artificial, instruments. They can fine-tune each aspect of a synthetic instrument's sound to give the app a unique feel.

Art directors control the overall look and feel of an app.

OVERSEEING APP ART

Larger development teams might rely on an art director to keep a watchful eye over all of the audio and visual aspects of an app. Art directors work with graphic designers, music composers, and other creative members of the team to make sure an app has a consistent appearance that meets the developers' goals. Art direction is a part of an app's overall UX design. As a result, a UX designer might also serve as a project's art director. ✳

Sound effects might come from a library of already existing sounds, or a team may create completely new sounds for an app.

Complex apps require a huge amount of code, and programmers work hard to find and fix any mistakes before an app's release.

SPEAKING A DIFFERENT LANGUAGE

A well-planned design isn't the only thing a new app needs to make the jump from an idea to a usable piece of software. Development teams need programmers to translate their plans into a language that mobile devices can understand. In many cases, a developer might handle those programming duties. However, larger development teams might have members who specialize exclusively in writing computer code. These skilled programmers are often familiar with several programming languages, and writing computer code is second nature to them. A talented programmer can spot any mistakes in code before they become bigger problems.

A programmer can also make sure an app runs as smoothly as possible on a wide range of different devices. Specialized quality assurance (QA) testers may take part in this process as well. They make sure an app meets its goals and runs smoothly, informing programmers about any glitches they experience.

GRAPHICS GURUS

As mobile devices become more powerful, many designers are taking advantage of the latest and greatest 3D graphics technology to add new functions and interesting visual designs. For example, many game apps feature vast 3D worlds filled with detailed character models. Games aren't the only apps using advanced 3D visuals, though. Google Earth offers a 3D model of our planet that can be turned and zoomed in all the way to street level. A number of apps allow users to explore 3D models showing the anatomy of the human body.

To create these graphics, app development teams employ the skills of talented 3D modelers and animators. 3D modelers use special software to build 3D objects out of **polygons**. Animators bring these objects to life by designing the way they move.

App graphics have to look nice, whether they appear on a small smartphone screen or a larger tablet or computer.

Nick Leonard is a user experience designer with Fuzzy Math, a company that designs and improves specialized apps and Web sites for clients such as GE Healthcare and RogerEbert.com.

When did you start thinking you wanted to be a designer? Did any person or event inspire that career choice? My interest in being a designer grew out of a general interest in computers and technology, and realizing the more I used different applications that many were very useful but difficult to use. I would think about how I'd want them to work and eventually realized that I could do just that as a profession.

What kinds of classes should a would-be designer look to take in middle school, high school, and beyond? Good design combines an understanding of technology, an understanding of the people who might use your app, and a critical eye to spot things that work well and those that don't. Classes in programming and robotics will help provide technical background, while many different creative classes, like art or writing, will help develop skills in creating things for other people.

What other projects and jobs did you do in school and your work life before the opportunity to work in app design came along? How did that work prepare you for your career? In college I studied journalism and worked at a newspaper, which was very helpful in learning how to write well and tell effective stories, which are both essential to communicate your design ideas to other team members. I also learned how to effectively interview people, which is a common research technique used in design to help learn about the people who might use your app.

Do you have a particular project that you're especially proud of or that you think really took your work to another level? I worked on a project for doctors, especially those in the ER, to be able to more quickly and easily scan a new patient's medical history. As part of this project, the rest of the design team and I went to hospitals and spoke with doctors, hearing many stories where an app like the one we were working on would be helpful. After finishing our designs, we took a **prototype** of our design to some of the doctors we'd talked to during research and who were excited to try out the prototype.

It takes teamwork to create an app. Does working as part of a team come naturally to you, or was it something you had to work on? I enjoy working with other people but also enjoy spending time by myself working on a design problem. Frequently, this means I'll do some design by myself at first to generate ideas, then work with other designers and developers and combine my ideas with theirs and work toward a final design.

If you had unlimited resources to work on any project you wanted to, what would you do? Once you start designing or building apps, you start realizing all kinds of things you want to make better or create a new app for. I think if I could work on anything, I'd want [to work] on something to help impoverished communities. These communities typically don't have the same access to technology as more affluent areas, providing a big design challenge but one that could make a big, positive impact.

What advice would you give a young person who wants to be a professional designer one day? Start any design project by understanding, in as much detail as you possibly can, the subject of your app and the people you think might use it. What solutions are out there today, and how can you improve upon those? Who will use your app, and what would make your app awesome for those people? It's tempting to rush to a final design, but taking the time to understand some background will result in a better overall design. ☀

IN THE CLASSROOM

App development is a field that is constantly growing and changing. The steady evolution of mobile technology means that app developers must constantly learn new skills to stay on the cutting edge of the industry. However, most developers begin their education with a similar group of basic skills. Whether or not they are in charge of writing code, they most likely have some background in computer programming. Even if a developer does not write code, he or she needs a basic understanding of how programming languages work in order to give instruction to programmers and review their work.

Most app developers hone their skills by attending college. They pursue degrees in subjects such as computer science, software engineering, or even math. In addition to classroom work, aspiring developers often seek **internships** with app development companies. These temporary jobs provide students with a firsthand look at the day-to-day realities of designing, building, and maintaining apps.

Universities offer a huge variety of classes and programs that can be applied to app development.

App design can start at any age.

AMATEUR APPS

If you're interested in creating apps as a career, or even just for fun, you don't need to wait to get started. Software developers of all kinds often begin learning the ropes at a very young age. Getting started with app development is as simple as downloading and installing a software development kit (SDK) on your computer. An SDK includes the tools needed to program an app, and free SDKs are available for both iOS and Android. Once you have an SDK installed, you can start creating your first app right away. Both Apple and Google offer in-depth online tutorials to help new users learn the basics of iOS or Android development. From there, you can practice and continue to learn new skills as you go. Don't worry if something doesn't work right on the first try or if you struggle to understand a new concept. These difficulties are normal for beginning developers, and solving your problems will give you a better understanding of how apps work.

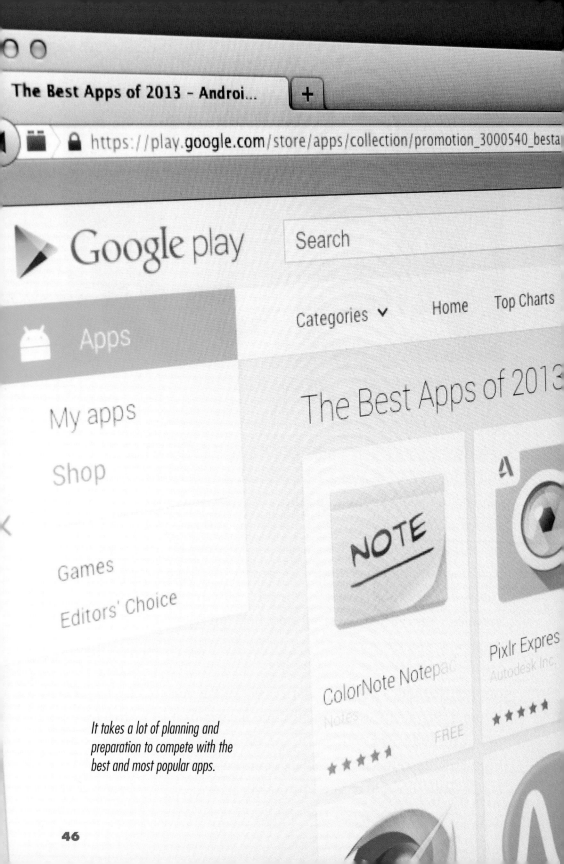

The Best Apps of 2013 – Androi...   +

https://play.google.com/store/apps/collection/promotion_3000540_besta

Google play

Search

Categories ∨   Home   Top Charts

Apps

My apps

Shop

The Best Apps of 2013

NOTE

Games

Editors' Choice

ColorNote Notepad
Notes

FREE

Pixlr Expres
Autodesk Inc.

★★★★★

It takes a lot of planning and preparation to compete with the best and most popular apps.

★★★★★

4

DEVELOPMENT DAYS

H undreds of new apps are released every day. Not all of them can be hits. There are so many options for users to choose from that perhaps only a few people download a new app. Some apps never receive any downloads at all. And while some apps are the product of small teams or individuals, large teams of professionals are behind many apps. These professionally created apps require time, money, and other resources to complete. As a result, professional app developers cannot afford to fail. They must carefully plan, build, and promote their apps to give them the best possible chance at catching on with a wide audience of mobile device owners.

MORE AND MORE APPS

July 2008	May 2014	June 2014	June 2014
The iOS App Store has around 500 total apps available.	Google's Gmail app becomes the first Android app ever to reach one billion total downloads.	Apple announces that more than 75 billion apps have been downloaded through the iOS App Store.	The iOS App Store and Google Play each have around 1.2 million apps available.

A new app might start with a discussion about how to solve an issue in everyday life.

STARTING POINTS

All apps start with a basic idea. Sometimes this might be as simple as someone using a favorite app and thinking of a way to make it better. Other times, it might be the result of a group of people getting together and discussing ideas for brand-new apps that are unlike anything seen before.

Many apps are created by developers who think their ideas can improve people's lives. They design apps out of a desire to simplify an everyday activity or create entirely new possibilities. Some apps are designed by businesses to offer convenient services to their customers. For example, a bank might offer an app that allows customers to manage their accounts, while an online store might have an app that makes it easier to purchase items on the go. Some apps are even designed to promote other products or businesses. For example, a television network might hire developers to build an app that plays video clips and displays news updates about one of its shows. Sometimes, a business might employ its own app development team. Other times, it might hire an independent team to do the job.

REFINING THE DESIGN

Once a development team knows what kind of app it will be making, it can begin planning the different features the app will include. The team works to make the app as useful as possible without going over budget or getting too far behind schedule. Development teams might be required to work with a very specific deadline and amount of money. If they plan features that are too ambitious, they might not be able to deliver their app on schedule.

Once the developers have a range of features in mind, they begin working with the design team to organize the app and make sure it will be easy to use. They try to create an **intuitive** UI so users do not have to spend much time learning how to access the app's various features. Developers might test out a few different design prototypes to see which one works best.

App designers brainstorm the functions and navigation of a new app.

WHERE THE MAGIC HAPPENS

One simple game solved a very big problem for Rovio Entertainment.

ROVIO ENTERTAINMENT

Established technology companies such as Google, Apple, and Microsoft create many popular and successful mobile apps. These companies have enormous resources to spend on app development, and people are more likely to download their apps because they recognize and trust the companies' names. However, much smaller developers create most apps. The creators work hard and experience modest success if they are lucky. But every once in a while, a small, independent app can take off, turning a small developer into a valuable company overnight. One of the biggest success stories in app history is Rovio Entertainment, the creators of the hugely popular mobile game *Angry Birds*.

TRY AND TRY AGAIN

Rovio was founded in 2003 by a small group of Finnish game developers who had attended college together. At the time, downloadable games and other apps were becoming more and more popular among mobile phone users. However, this was before the days of easy-to-use app stores and smartphone operating systems. It was difficult to create games that worked on a wide variety of devices and to make them available to a wide audience. The company created dozens of games during its first few years, but they did not bring in enough money to make Rovio a success. By 2009, the company had only a few employees and was almost bankrupt.

Rovio's Henri Holm (center) and Paul Chen (right) talk with Angry Birds fans.

A HIT AT LAST

Rovio's leaders knew that the company was in trouble, but they had a plan to save it. After seeing the successful launch of the iOS App Store, they realized there was finally an easy way to release their games to a larger audience. They began looking at the things that other successful mobile games had in common. Their new game would need colorful characters that could appeal to both kids and adults. It would also need to be fun in short bursts. Rovio's Jaakko Iisalo came up with an idea for a game in which players tried to destroy buildings and defeat enemies by launching bird characters at them with a slingshot. The team worked at the game for several months and finally released it

Rovio has developed several variations on Angry Birds, *including* Angry Birds Star Wars.

to the iOS App Store in December 2009. *Angry Birds* was not a hit at first. However, Rovio worked hard to promote the game, and word began to spread among iPhone users throughout the world. By the following spring, *Angry Birds* had become a massive worldwide success, and Rovio was no longer in danger of going out of business.

LOOKING FORWARD

Since its success on iOS, *Angry Birds* has been released on a variety of other mobile operating systems and video game consoles. Rovio has also released several sequels and spin-offs to its signature hit. Each one has been a huge success. Today, there are *Angry Birds* cartoons, toys, and even theme parks. In 2014, Rovio released its first non-*Angry Birds* game in several years. Called *Retry*, it features a style of gameplay similar to the hit *Flappy Bird*. Players control an airplane and try to avoid obstacles by tapping the screen. Only time will tell if Rovio has another hit on its hands. ✺

CATCHING EYES

As the development team works on features and UI design, it is also working hard to come up with ideas for the app's final appearance. Developers, designers, and artists work together to choose colors, shapes, and animations. They sort through libraries of fonts to find just the right ones. They create **mock-ups** to see how these different pieces fit together to form a complete package.

If the team has been hired to create an app for another company, it might have to present several different design ideas to the clients. The team might also have specific restrictions. For example, a company might have official colors and logos that need to be included in the app. Developers who are working for themselves have more room to make their own creative decisions. However, they must keep their audience in mind and make design decisions that will attract as many new users as possible.

Several people might review and adjust a design before it is finalized.

Good programming enables people to use and enjoy an app.

CRANKING OUT CODE

Programming is not as simple as converting ideas into software. It is a continual process of writing and revising code to improve an app. This means searching through code to find errors or ways to **optimize** the app and make it run faster and more reliably. Programmers work to make sure all of an app's features function the way they are supposed to. They also try to make sure that the app will run on as many different devices as possible so it will be available to more people. Not all users upgrade to the latest devices every year, so apps that won't run on older devices are unlikely to reach as many people. Programmers also have an impact on how smoothly an app runs. Optimizing code can lead to shorter load times and prevent crashes.

LASTING CONTRIBUTIONS

GPS can keep track of every place you took a photo on vacation.

WHERE ON EARTH?

Many of today's top mobile apps rely on GPS technology for some of their most amazing features. With GPS, apps can pinpoint a device's location almost anywhere on Earth. This is useful in an incredible number of situations. A camera app might use GPS to mark photos with the location where they were taken, so users won't have to make their own notes. An app for finding movie showtimes might automatically notice where the user is and search the nearest theaters. GPS can even help people track lost or stolen devices by

logging onto a Web site and tracking the missing item remotely. GPS might seem like advanced, cutting-edge technology, but it was actually invented decades ago!

HOW DOES IT WORK?

GPS stands for "global positioning system." It relies on a system of at least 24 satellites in orbit around Earth. The satellites travel around the planet twice per day, and they are arranged so that several are always in range of every point on Earth's surface.

The GPS devices we use are called receivers. These devices send signals to the

A single GPS satellite completes two orbits around Earth each day.

Some GPS units are made especially for hikers. They show terrain instead of roads.

satellites in orbit above, and the satellites respond. By measuring its own distance from at least four satellites, a GPS receiver can calculate its position on Earth's surface.

A LONG HISTORY

The first human-made satellite, *Sputnik I*, went into orbit in 1957. Almost immediately, engineers began experimenting with using satellites to create navigation systems. In 1959, the U.S. Navy launched a satellite navigation system for locating submarines. It took hours for people aboard the sub to receive signals back from the satellites above.

By the mid-1970s, the U.S. military had begun launching test satellites for what would become today's GPS system. The first fully operational GPS satellite was launched in 1989, and all 24 were in orbit by 1995. Three additional satellites

were also launched as spares in case one of the original satellites malfunctioned. Since then, several new satellites have been added, and old ones have been replaced. Today, there are 31 GPS satellites circling the planet.

At first, only the U.S. government used the GPS system. However, restrictions on the system's use have lessened over time. While the government still regulates some uses of GPS, the technology is open for almost anyone to use today. The first GPS-equipped phone was released in 1999. As the technology grew less expensive and more compact, it began to be included in many more devices. Today, almost all smartphones and tablets have GPS receivers built in. Many people also purchase dedicated GPS receivers to help them navigate while driving. ✳

Last minute problems, such as program glitches or disapproval from beta testers or app stores, can be aggravating.

FINISHING TOUCHES

As an app nears completion, the team prepares for release by working to find and eliminate any bugs. In addition to testing the app in-house, the team might offer a public beta test. During this testing process, an early version of the app is provided for free to a group of users. In return, the users report any problems they have with the app. This allows the team to see how the app will work on a wide variety of devices and in different situations.

Once the team has a version of the app that it is satisfied with, it must submit it to app stores for approval. Major app stores such as Google Play and the iOS App Store have strict standards that apps must pass before they are put up for download. For example, apps will not be approved if they have too many bugs or often crash. They must also be free of offensive content. If an app is rejected, the team must fix its problems before submitting it again.

LAUNCH DAY

Once the new app is approved, the team works to spread the word and get people excited to download it. The team might advertise on popular Web sites or start conversations about the app on popular social networks such as Facebook or Twitter. With any luck, there will be a group of people interested in downloading the app as soon as it is released. If the app is a success, these early users will tell their friends about it. Many apps become well known through this type of word-of-mouth exposure.

Development doesn't end as soon as a new app goes live. The process of optimizing and adding new features continues even after an app is released. With thousands or even millions of people downloading an app, chances are high that users will discover new bugs that the development team never noticed. In addition, these users might request new features based on how they are using the app. The developers might also think up new ideas of their own. By continuing to support their apps long after their initial release, the developers build their reputation among mobile device users. As they get ready to start another project, they know that there is a loyal audience waiting to see what they'll think of next.

Developers know they've found success when users are excited about a new app.

THE FUTURE

GOOGLE GLASS CAN WORK
WITH PRESCRIPTION LENSES

A man holds up his smartphone, which shows what he sees through his Google Glass.

APPS EVERYWHERE

Now that apps have become an important part of the way people use phones and other mobile devices, engineers and software developers are working on ways to bring the functionality and convenience of apps to other everyday objects. There might come a day in the future when almost everything you use is controlled by apps, from the lights or appliances in your home to the ignition of your car. All of these devices would be connected to each other wirelessly, allowing you to access and control them from your mobile device.

HANDS FREE

One of the most talked-about new mobile devices of the past few years has been Google Glass. This tiny computer is worn like a pair of glasses. A small screen located right in front of the user's eye displays text, photos, and other information. Users can control the device through voice commands or, if they prefer, by using a small touch pad located on its side. Like a smartphone or a tablet, Google Glass can run a variety of apps, including programs for sending messages, taking photos and videos, and GPS navigation. Many app developers are excited by the possibilities of a completely hands-free mobile device. If Google Glass or a similar device takes off with the general public, you can expect a wide range of creative new apps to hit the market.

WEARABLE APPS

Many experts also expect "smart watches" to become a popular way of using apps. Though similar devices have existed for many years, computer technology has only recently become advanced enough for watches to offer the same sort of functionality as a smartphone in such a small package. Like other mobile devices, smart watches can access the Internet and run a variety of apps. They can also connect to smartphones to give users a quick way to access information without having to get out their phones. Manufacturers such as Samsung, Motorola, and Apple have all created their own takes on the smart watch. It remains to be seen if these devices will become as popular as smartphones or tablets, but they certainly have potential. ☀

Smart watches may one day become a standard way to browse the Internet, accomplish tasks, and make phone calls.

CAREER STATS

SOFTWARE DEVELOPERS

MEDIAN ANNUAL SALARY (2012): $93,350

NUMBER OF JOBS (2012): 1,018,000

PROJECTED JOB GROWTH: 22%, much faster than average

PROJECTED INCREASE IN JOBS 2012–2022: 222,600

REQUIRED EDUCATION: Bachelor's degree

LICENSE/CERTIFICATION: None

COMPUTER PROGRAMMERS

MEDIAN ANNUAL SALARY (2012): $74,280

NUMBER OF JOBS (2012): 343,700

PROJECTED JOB GROWTH: 8%, as fast as average

PROJECTED INCREASE IN JOBS 2012–2022: 28,400

REQUIRED EDUCATION: Bachelor's degree

LICENSE/CERTIFICATION: None

GRAPHIC DESIGNERS

MEDIAN ANNUAL SALARY (2012): $44,150

NUMBER OF JOBS (2012): 259,500

PROJECTED JOB GROWTH: 7%, slower than average

PROJECTED INCREASE IN JOBS 2012–2022: 17,400

REQUIRED EDUCATION: Bachelor's degree

LICENSE/CERTIFICATION: None

Figures reported by the United States Bureau of Labor Statistics

RESOURCES

BOOKS

Cunningham, Kevin. *Computer Graphics*. New York: Children's Press, 2013.

Gregory, Josh. *Steve Jobs*. New York: Children's Press, 2013.

Sirota, Lyn A. *Technological Design*. Ann Arbor, MI: Cherry Lake Publishing, 2012.

FACTS FOR NOW

Visit this Scholastic Web site for more information on apps:
www.factsfornow.scholastic.com
Enter the keyword **Apps**

GLOSSARY

cellular (SEL-yuh-lur) of or having to do with cell phones and their technology

conducts (kuhn-DUHKTS) allows heat, electricity, or sound to pass through

developer (di-VEL-uhp-ur) a person or company that creates computer software

engineer (en-juh-NEER) a person who is specially trained to design and build machines, large structures, or computer software and hardware

GPS (GEE PEE ESS) a system of satellites and devices that people use to find out where they are or to get directions to a place; GPS is short for "global positioning system"

hardware (HAHRD-wair) computer equipment

interfaces (IN-tur-fay-siz) the points at which two different things meet; for example, a keyboard is an interface between a computer and a user

internships (IN-turn-ships) programs allowing a student to learn a skill or job by working with an expert in his or her chosen field

intuitive (in-TOO-i-tiv) readily learned or understood

mock-ups (MAHK-ups) models of a machine or program that are used to study, test, or show its features

multitasking (MUHL-tee-task-ing) doing two or more things at the same time

networks (NET-wurks) groups of connected computers or communications equipment

operating systems (AH-pur-ay-ting SIS-tuhmz) software in computers or other devices that support all the programs that run on them

optimize (AHP-ti-mize) make as good or effective as possible

polygons (PAH-li-gahnz) shapes with three or more sides; triangles, squares, pentagons, and hexagons are all polygons

programming languages (PROH-gram-ing LANG-wij-iz) the coded languages in which instructions for a machine are written

prototype (PROH-tuh-tipe) the first version of an invention that tests an idea to see if it will work

software (SAWFT-wair) computer programs that control the workings of the equipment, or hardware, and direct it to do specific tasks

stylus (STYE-luhs) a small stick used like a pen to input data to some devices

viral (VYE-rul) quickly and widely spread

INDEX

Page numbers in *italics* indicates illustrations.

INDEX

ABOUT THE AUTHOR

JOSH GREGORY writes and edits books for kids. He lives in Chicago, Illinois.